Comparing

Taller

Which is taller, A or B? Circle the answer.

A	B	A	B

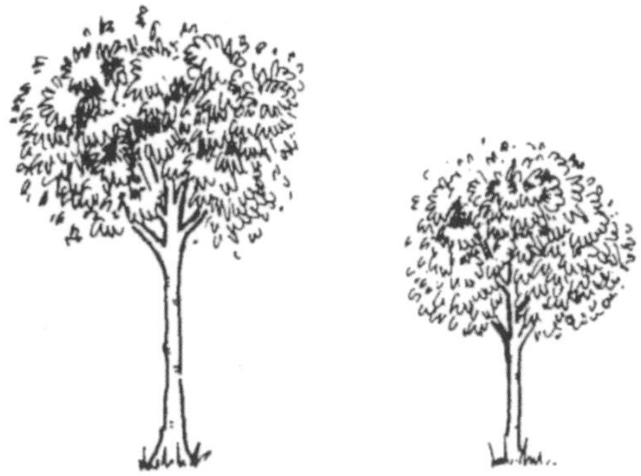

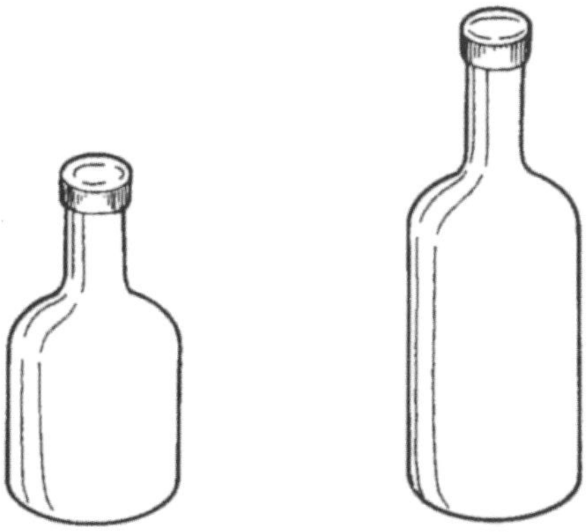

A	B	A	B

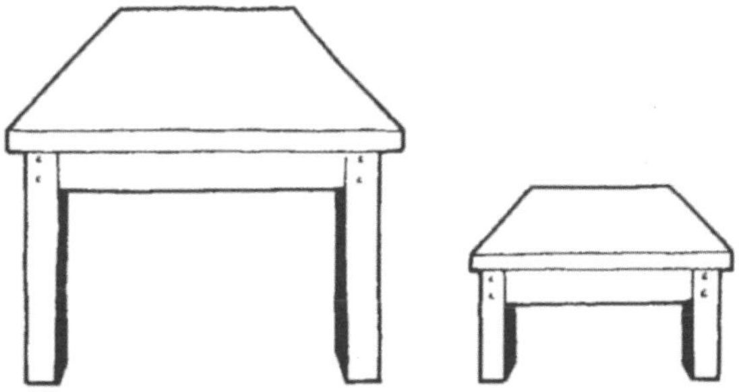

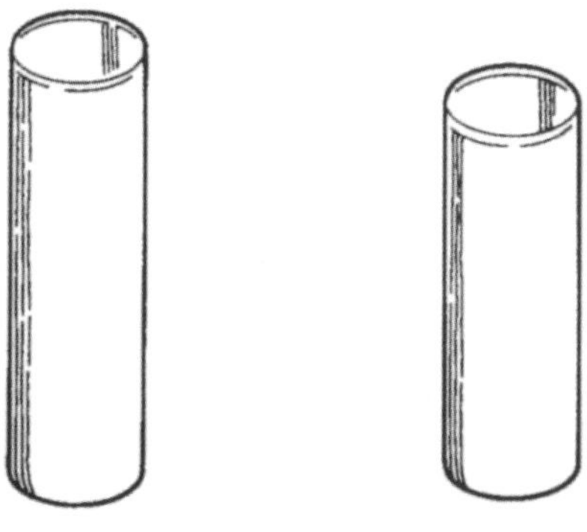

A	B	A	B

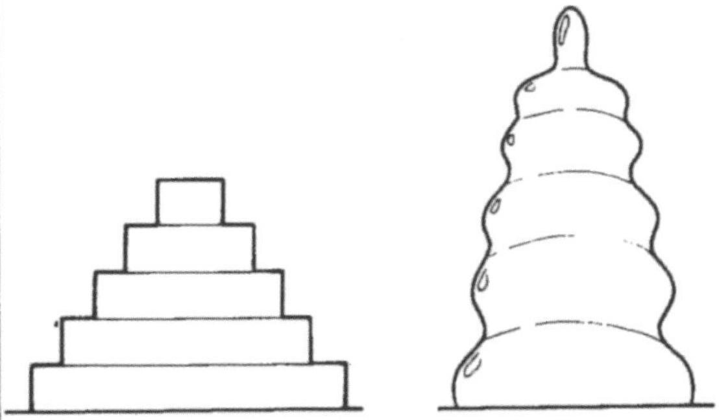

Shorter

Who is shorter, A or B? Circle the answer.

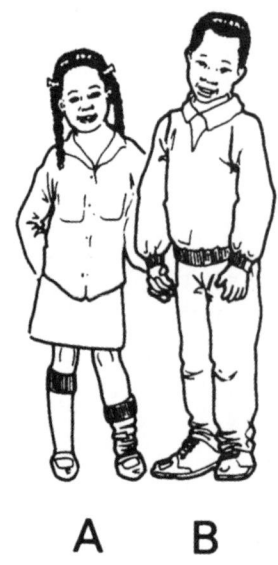

A B

A B

Longer

Which is longer, A or B? Circle the answer.

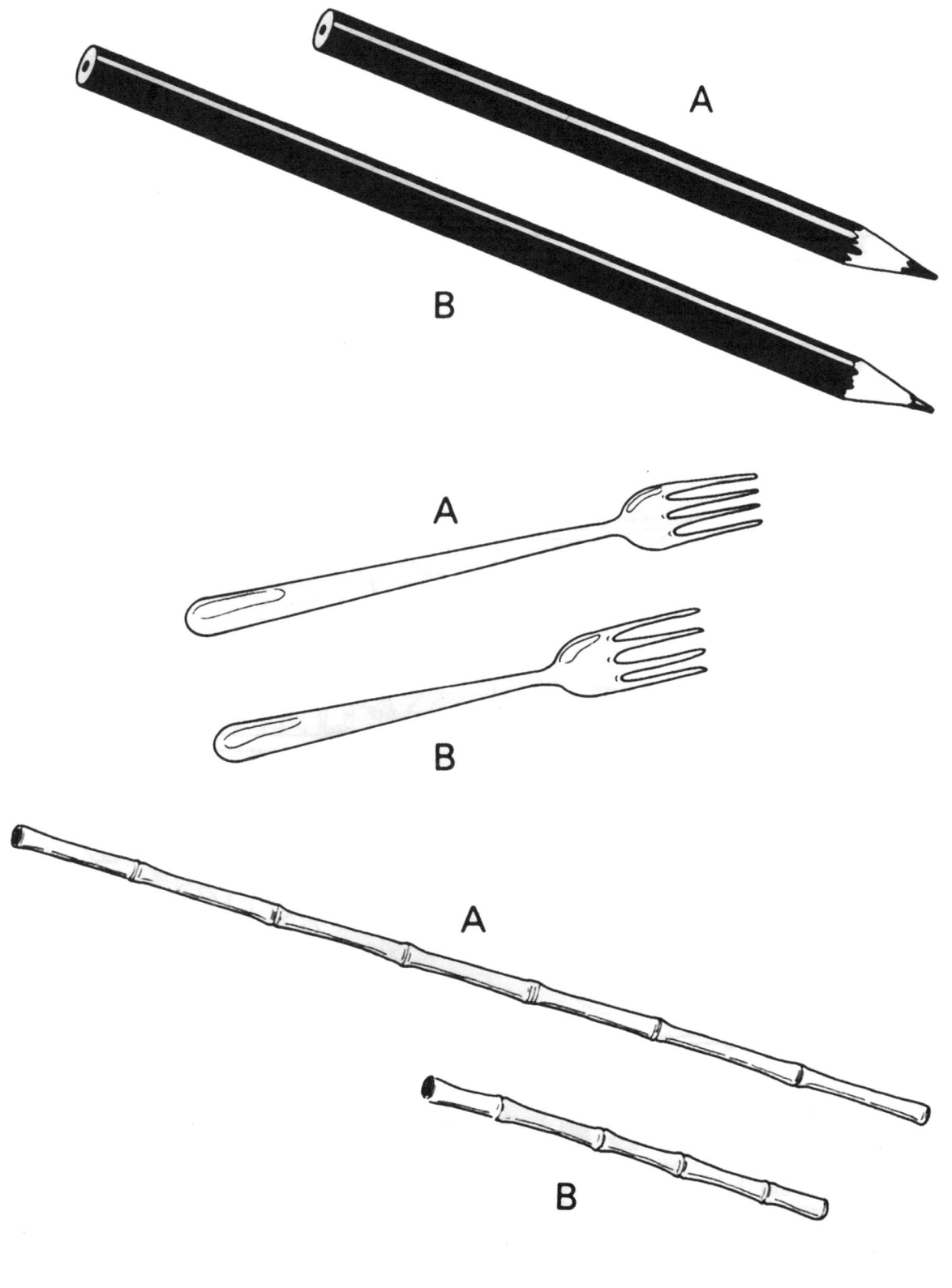

Shorter

Which is shorter, A or B? Circle the answer.

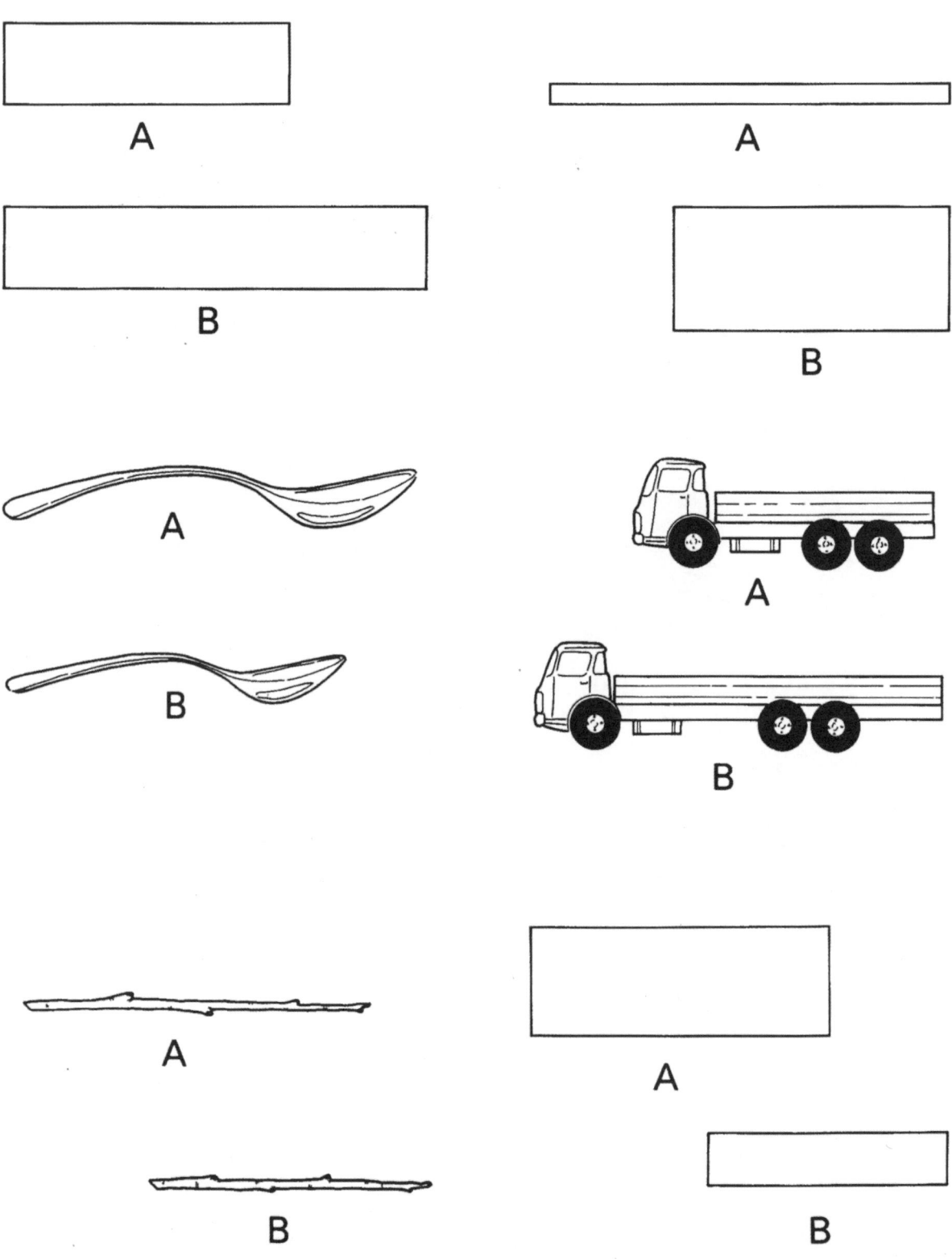

Bigger

Which is bigger, A or B? Circle the answer.

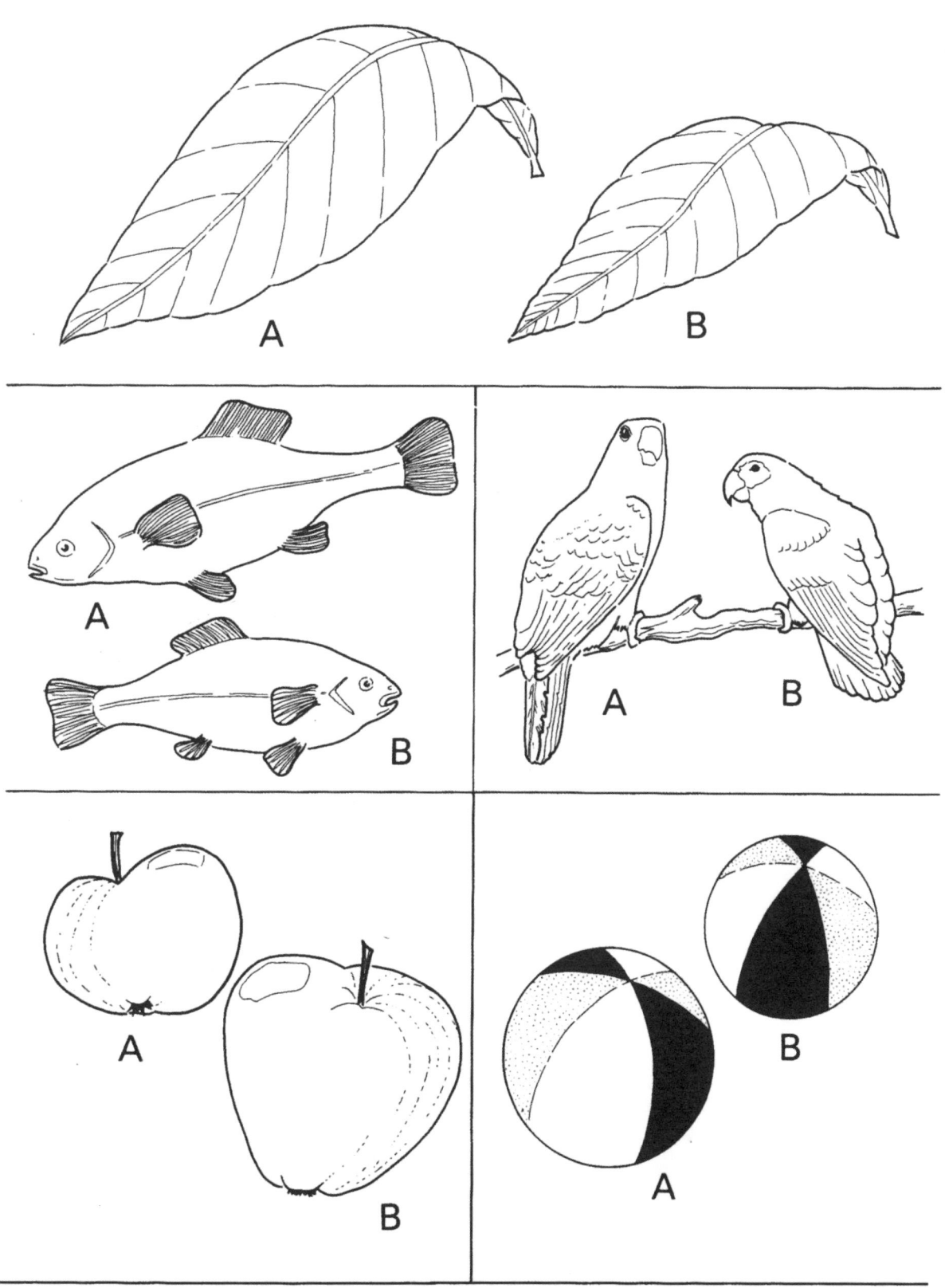

Smaller

Which is smaller, A or B? Circle the answer.

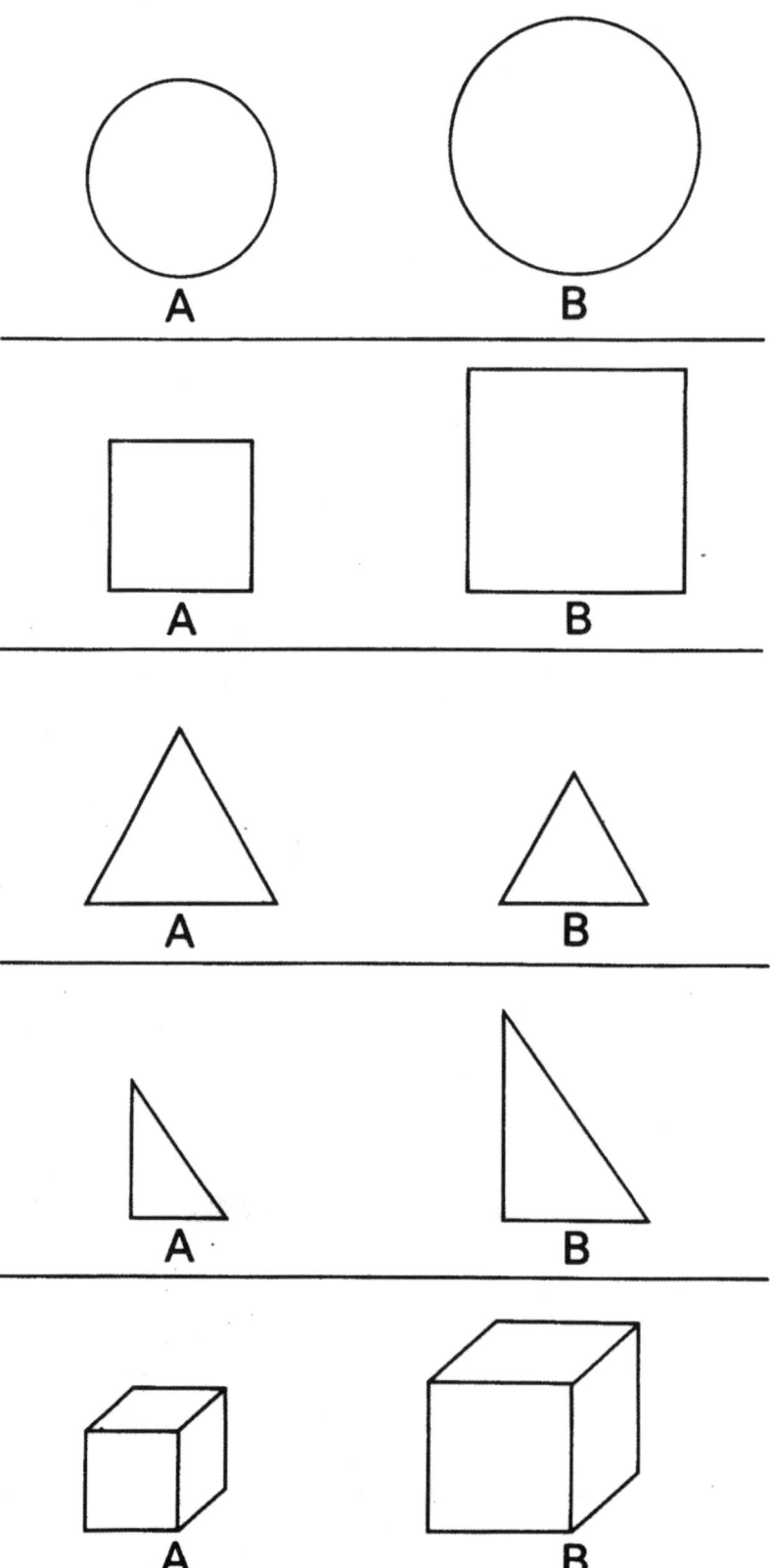

More

Which holds more, A or B? Circle the answer.

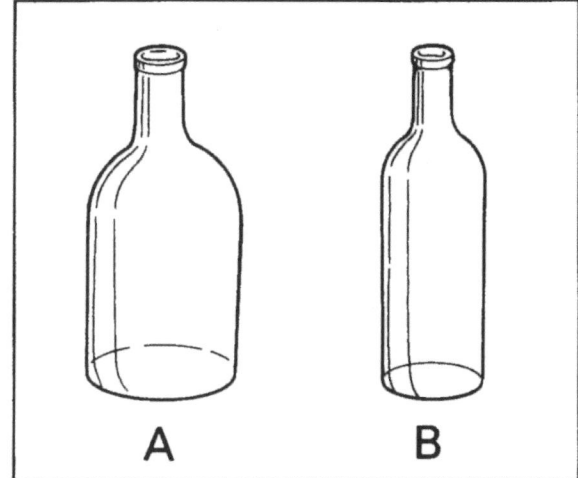
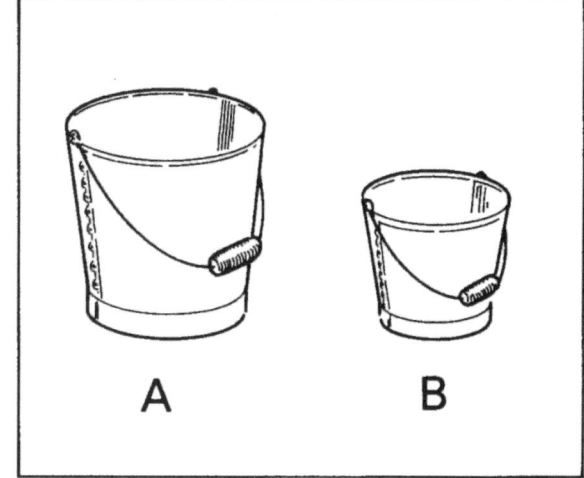
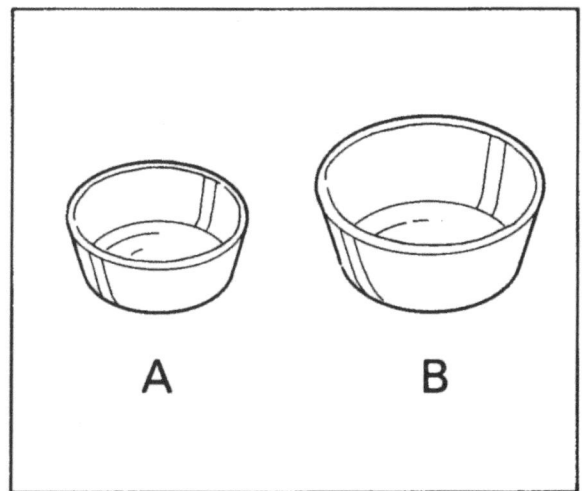
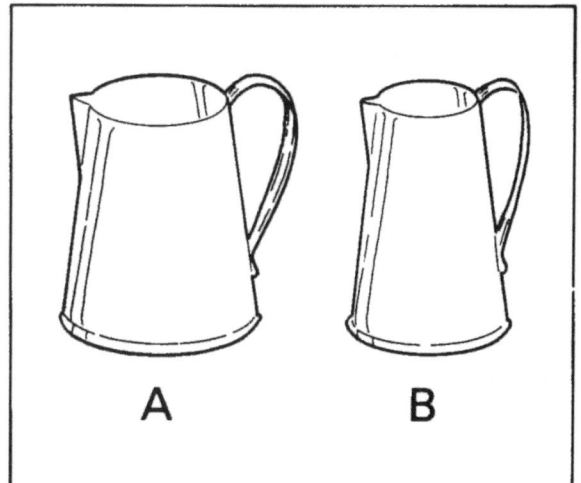
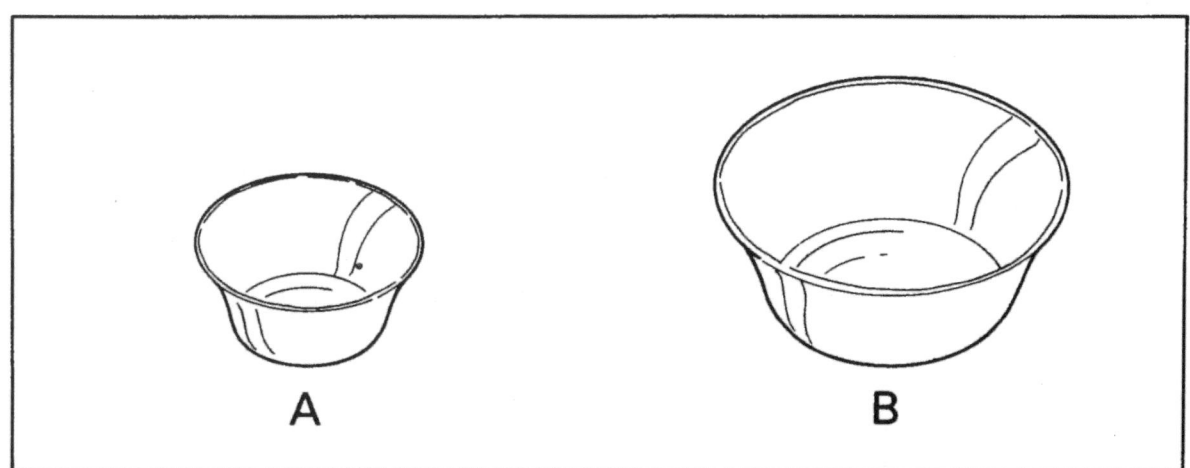

Less

Which holds less, A or B? Circle the answer.

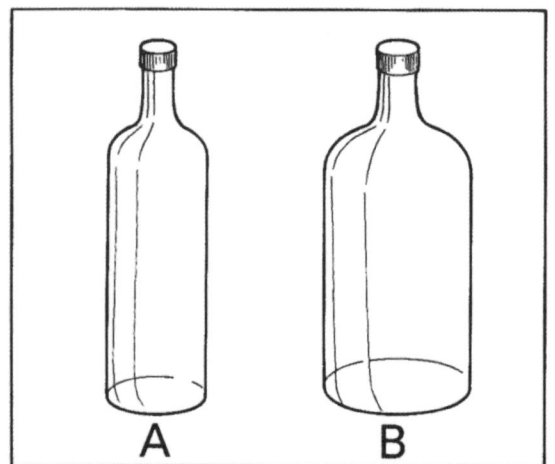
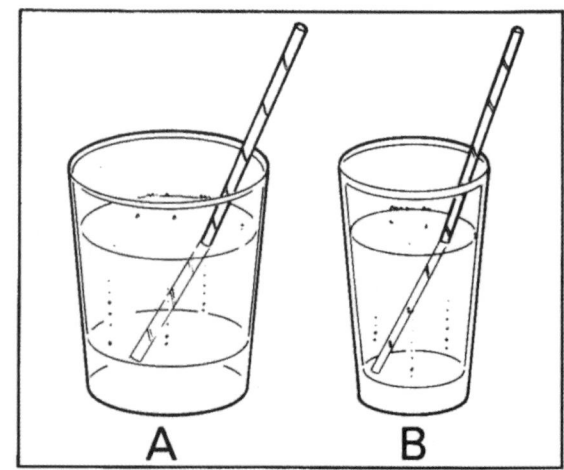
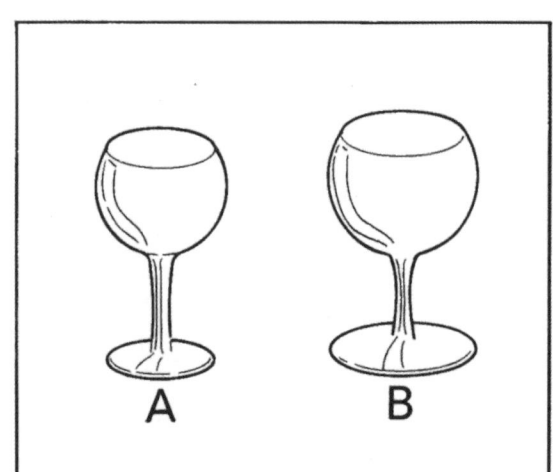

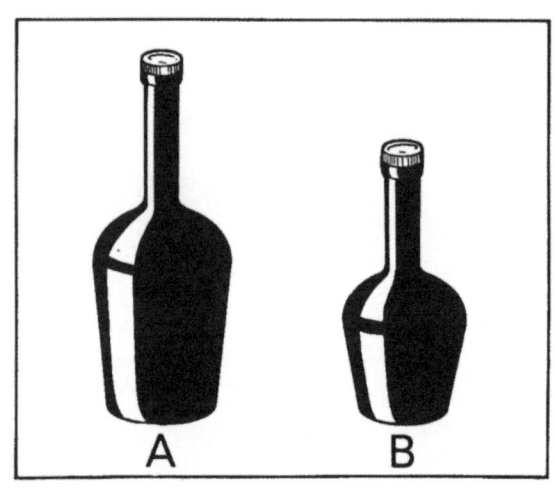

Shapes

The square

This is a square.

Colour all the squares.

The circle

This is a circle.

Colour all the circles.

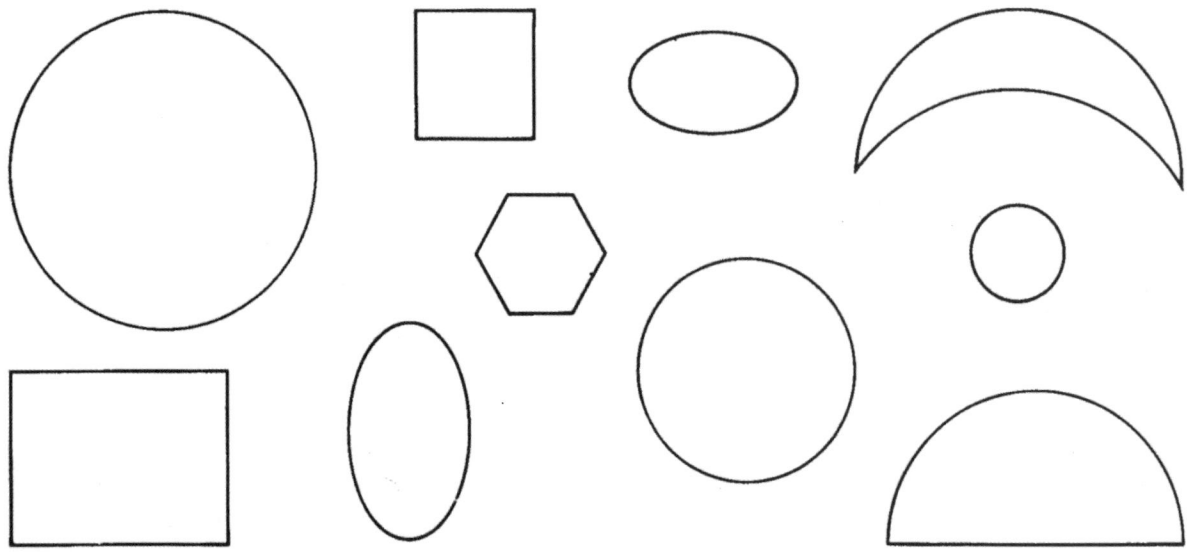

The triangle

This is a triangle.

Colour all the triangles.

Recognising 0, 1, 2, 3

0   1   2   3

How many?

Counting to 3

Count.

0   1   2   ☐

Matching numbers to objects

Match these numbers to the objects.

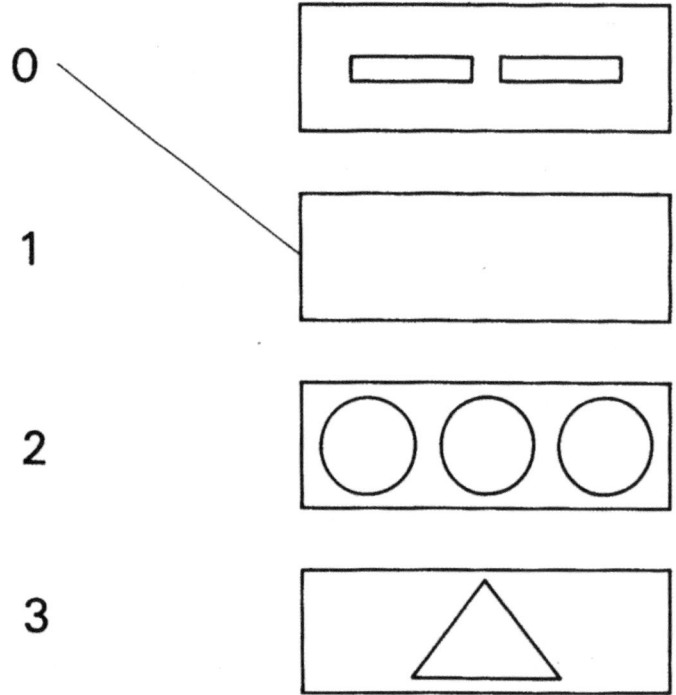

Spelling numbers up to 3

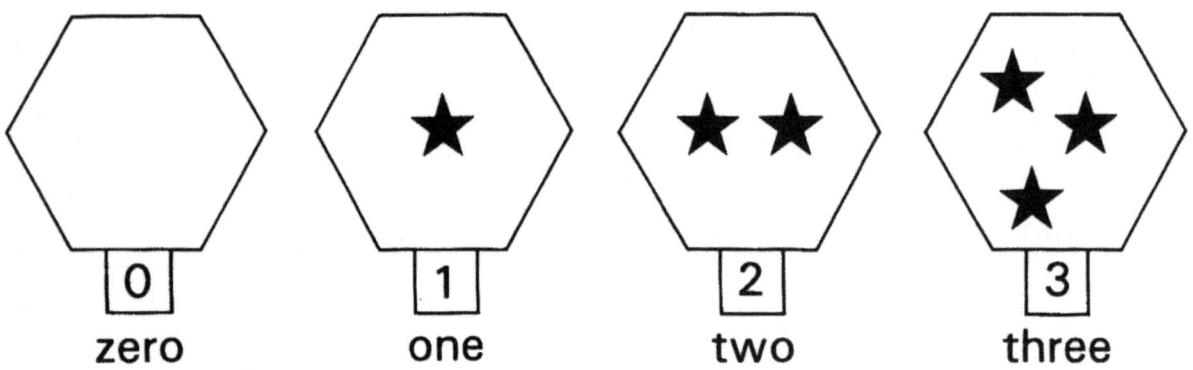

Writing numbers up to 3

Write these numbers.

three =   one =

zero =   two =

Recognising 4 and 5

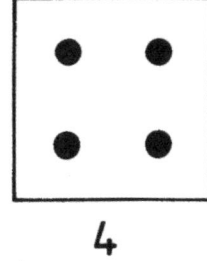
4

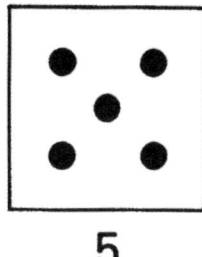
5

How many?

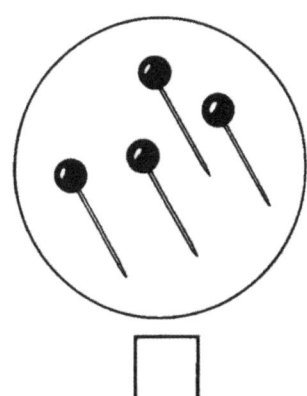
☐

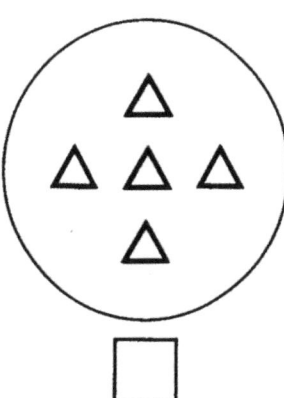
☐

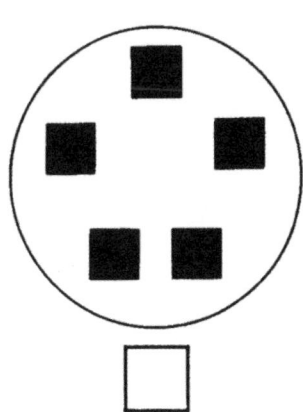
☐

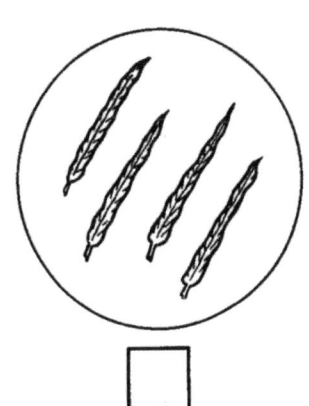
☐

Counting to 5

Count.

0   1   2   3   ☐   ☐

How many?

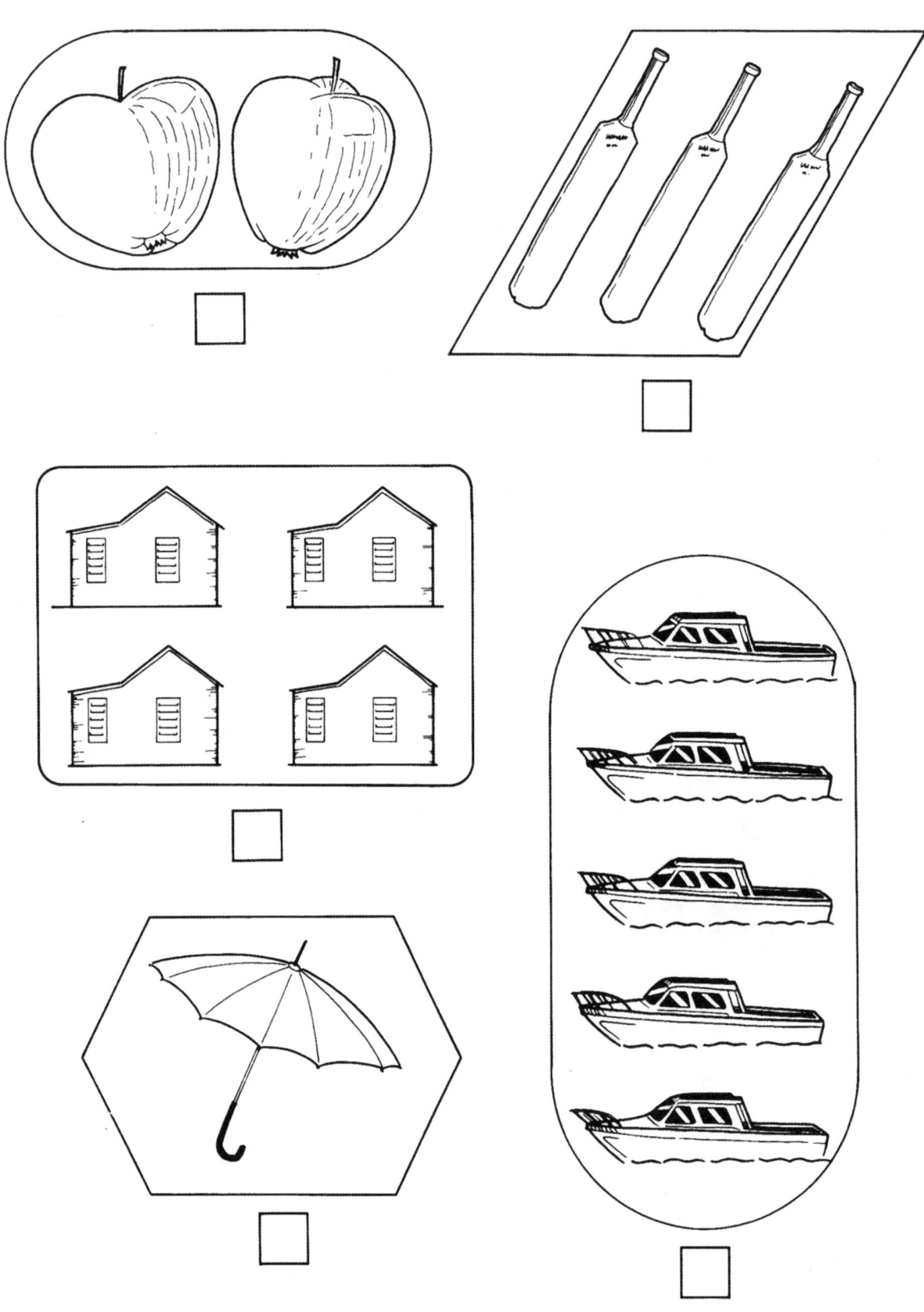

Matching numbers to objects

Match these numbers to the objects.

0

1

2

3

4

5

Spelling numbers 4 and 5

4

four

5

five

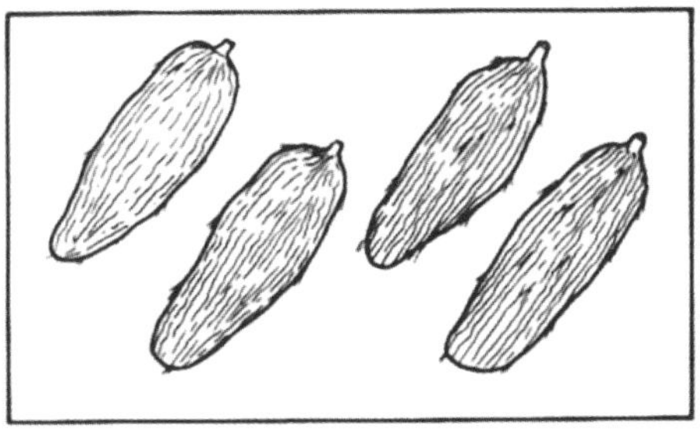

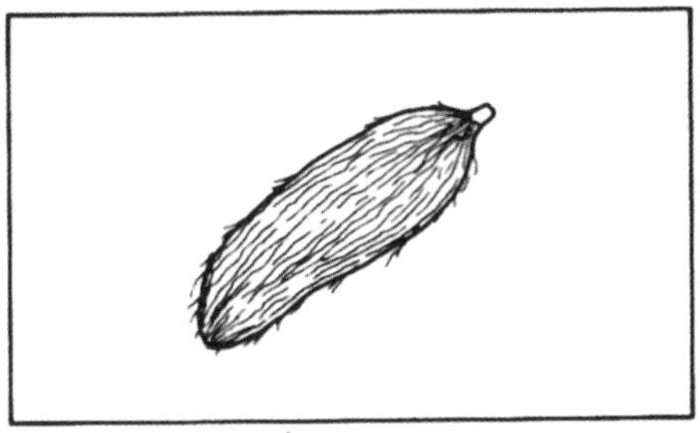

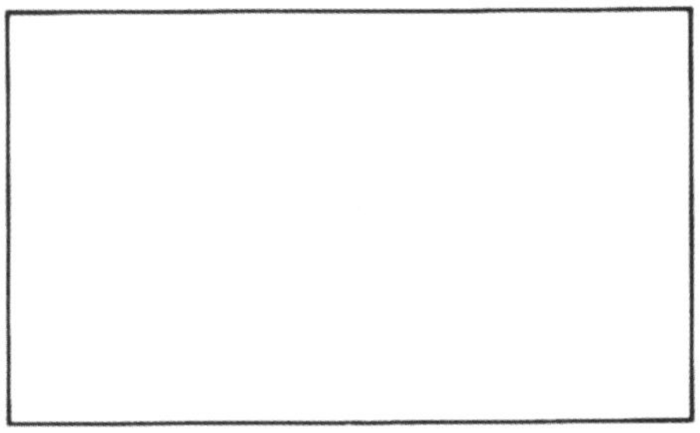

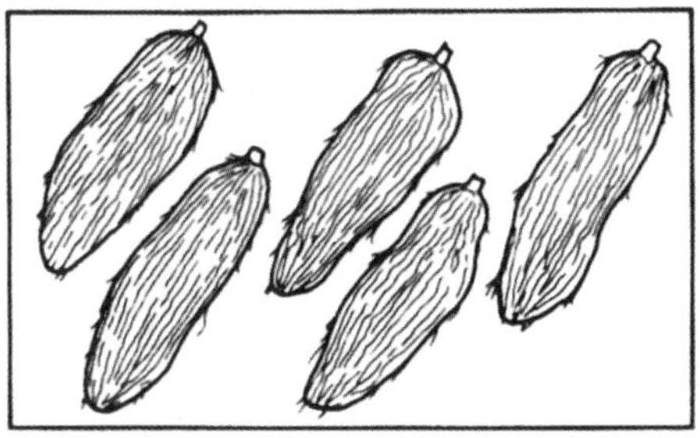

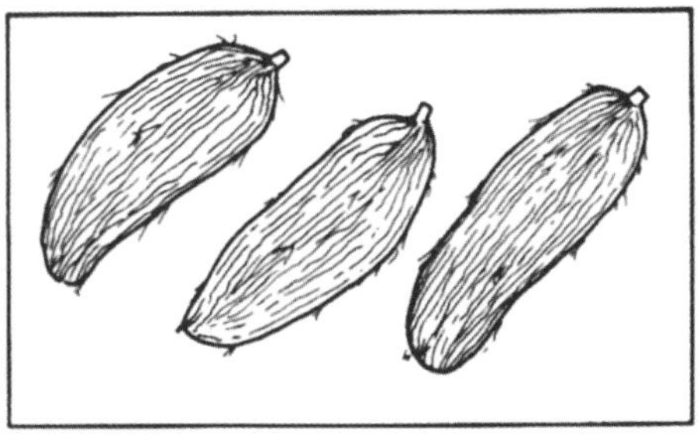

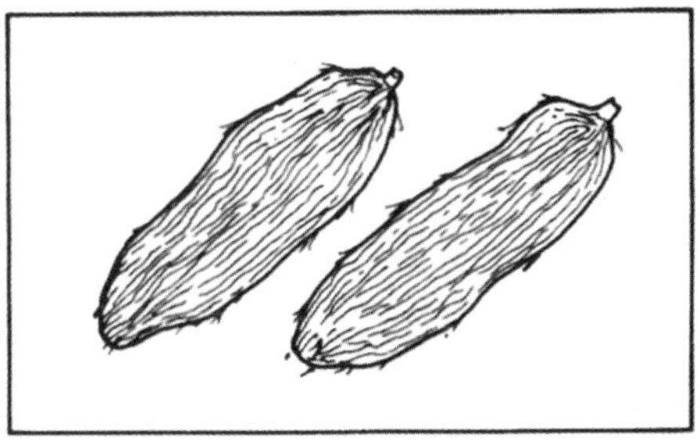

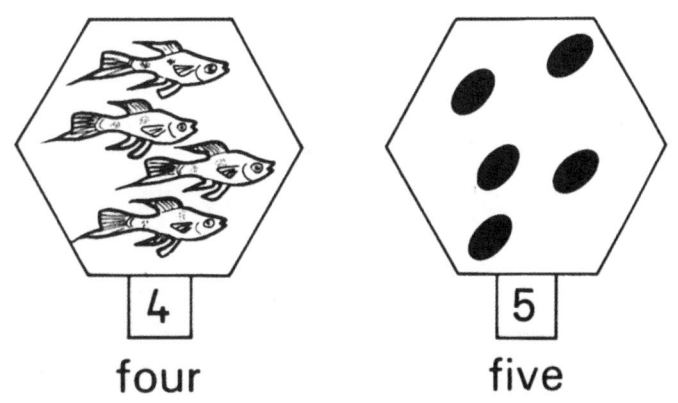

Drawing objects up to 5

Draw the number of objects in each circle.

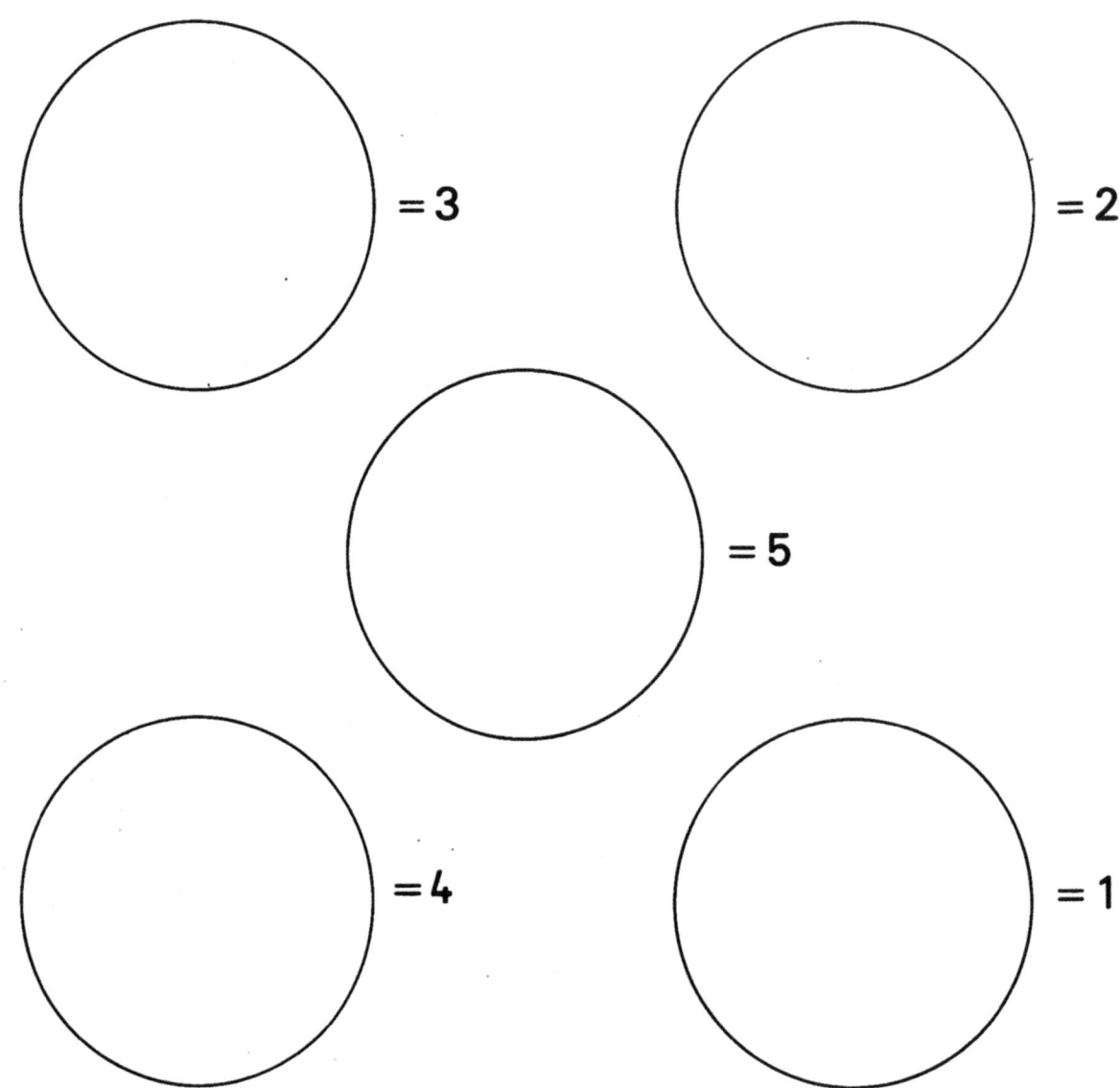

Writing numbers up to 5

Write these numbers.

two =   three =

five =   zero =

one =   four =

16

Recognising 6 and 7

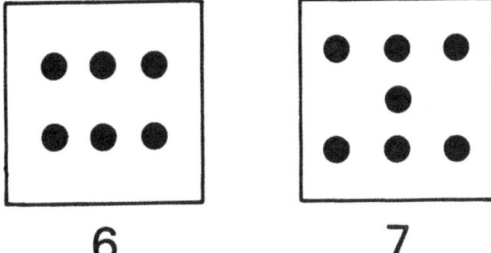

How many?

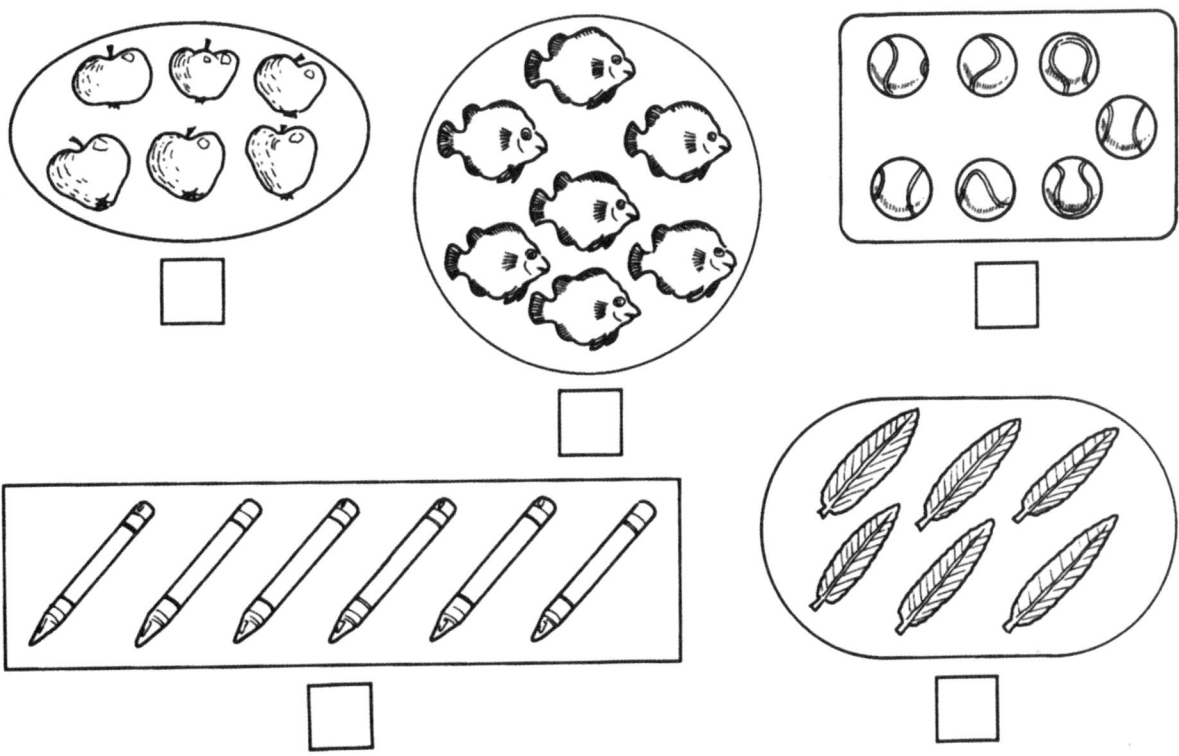

Spelling numbers 6 and 7

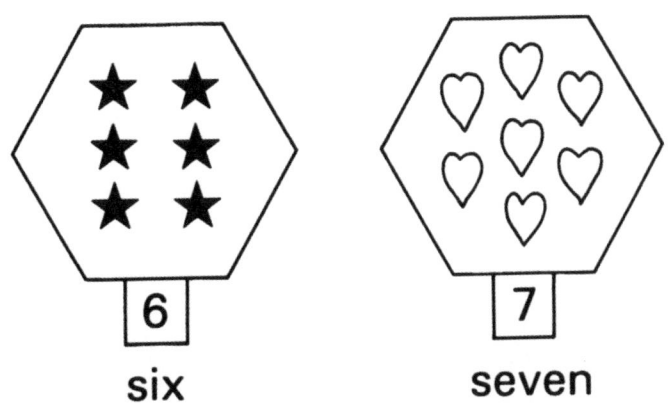

six   seven

How many?

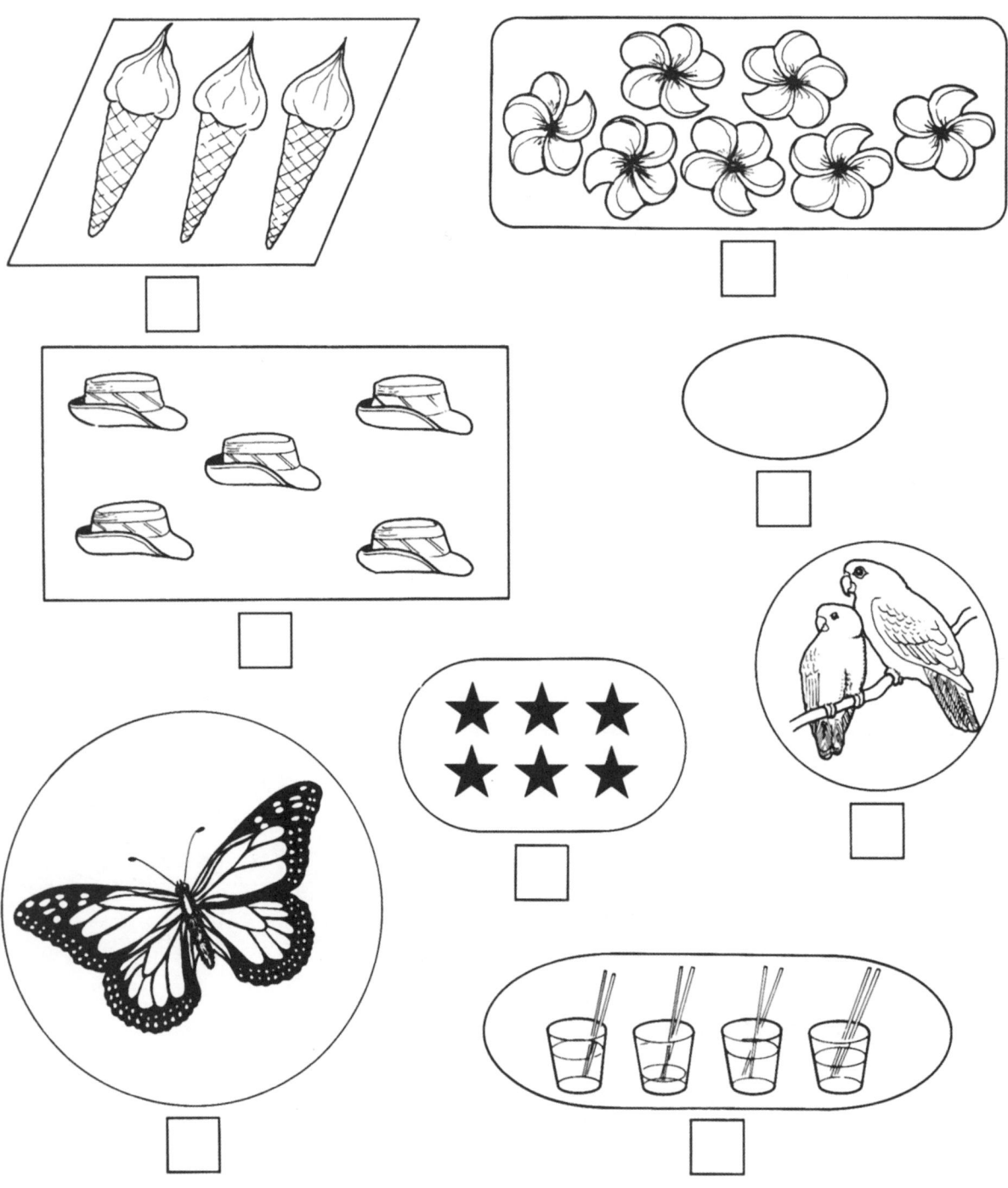

Counting to 7

Count.

0   1   2   ☐   4   5   ☐   ☐

Drawing objects up to 7

Draw the number of objects in each circle.

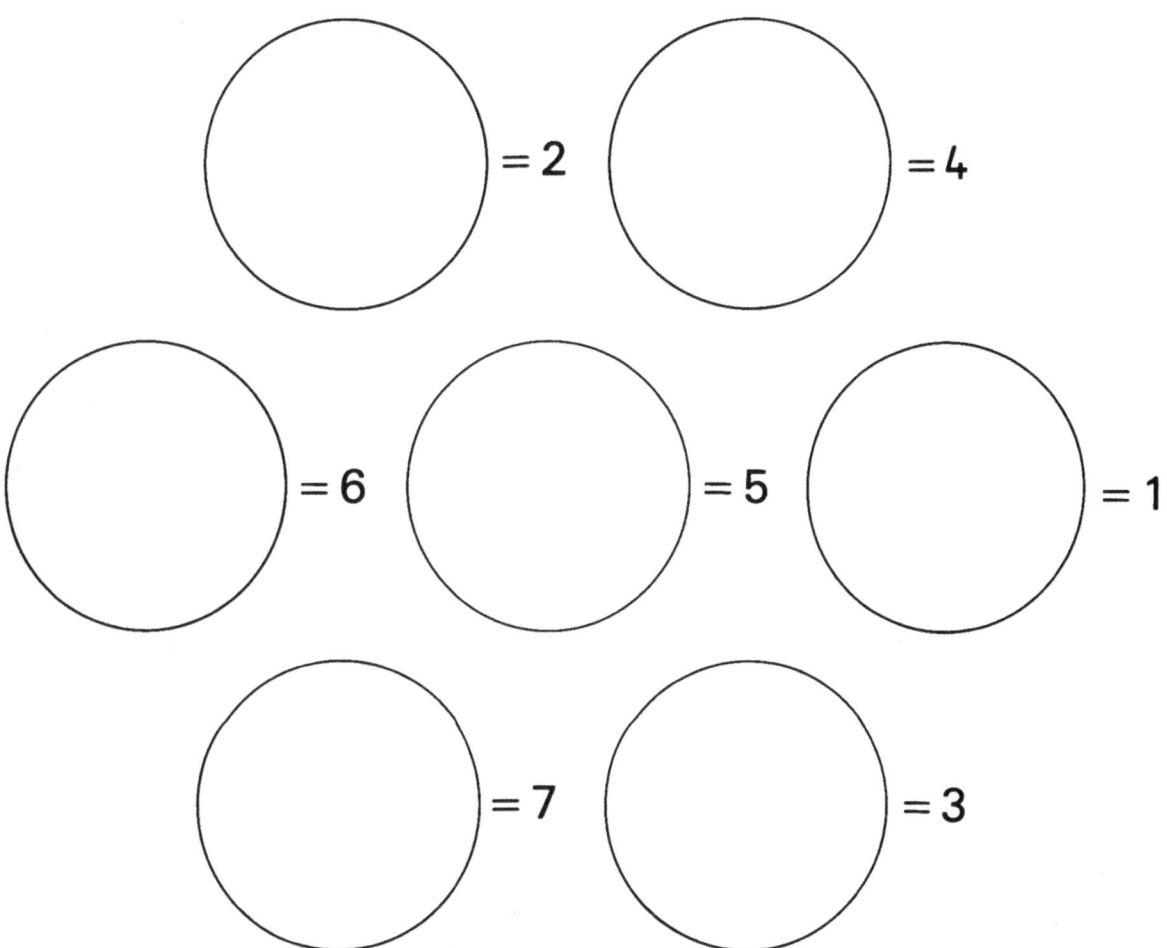

Matching numbers

Match these numbers by drawing a line.

3	six
2	three
5	zero
6	two
0	five
1	four
7	one
4	seven

Recognising 8 and 9

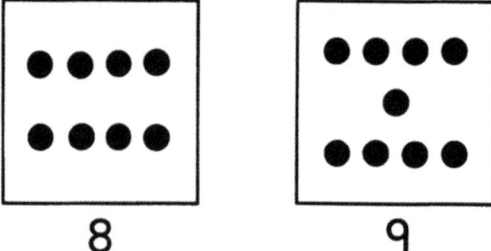

How many?

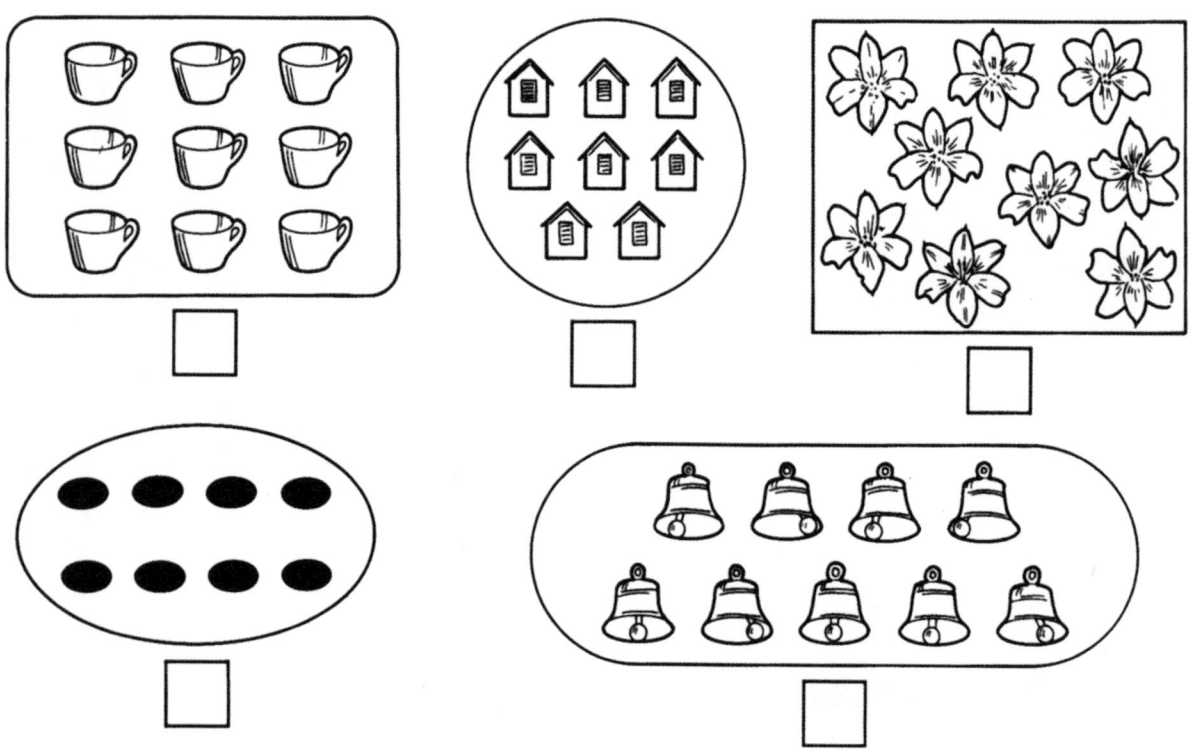

Spelling numbers 8 and 9

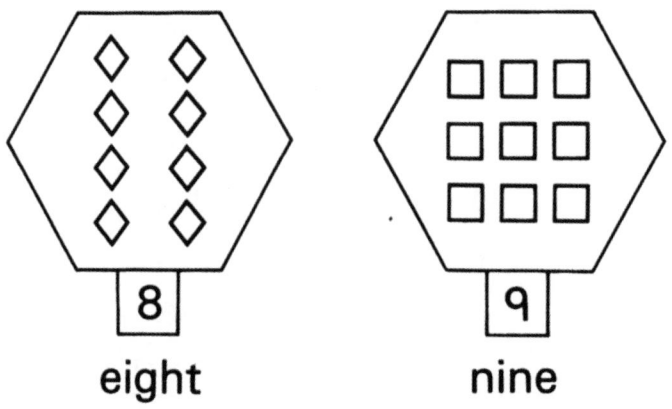

How many?

Counting to 9

Count.

0   1   2   3   ☐   5   6   7   ☐   ☐

21

Writing numbers up to 9

Write these numbers.

three   =   nine   =

five   =   two   =

eight   =   six   =

zero   =   four   =

one   =   seven   =

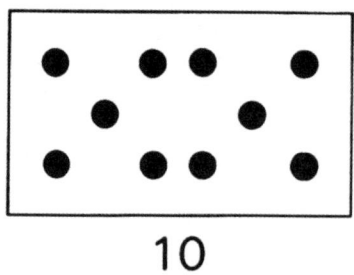

Recognising 10

10

How many? Circle the answer.

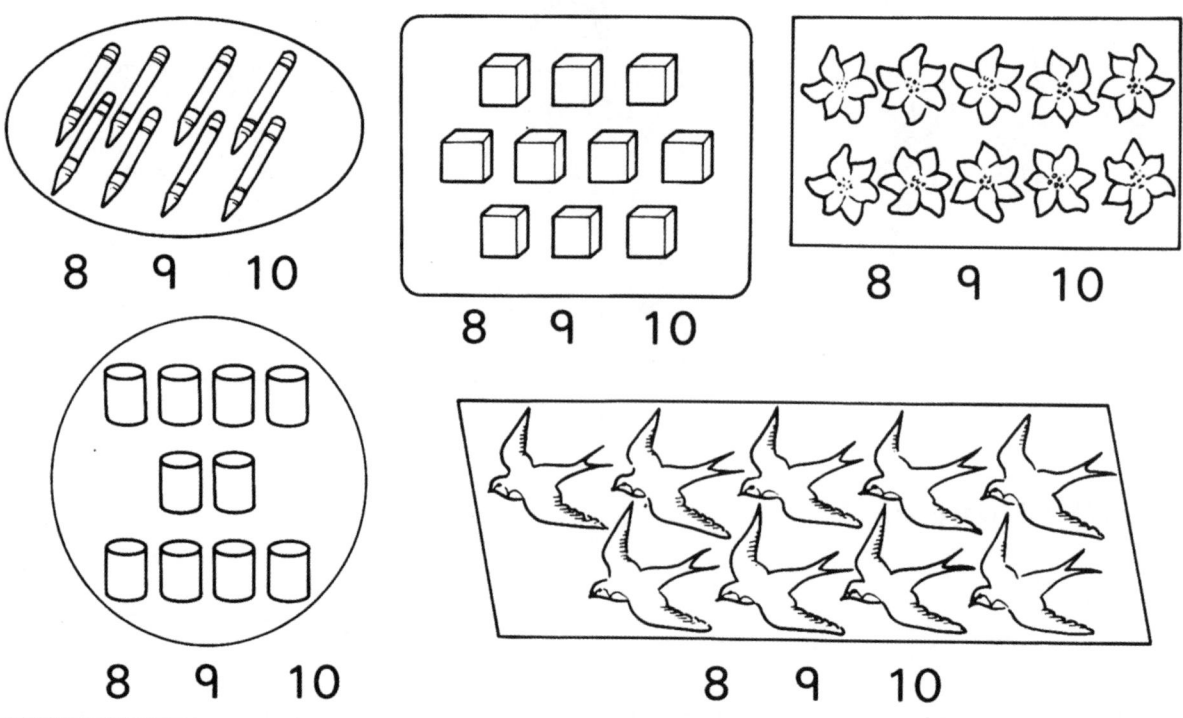

8   9   10

8   9   10

8   9   10

8   9   10

8   9   10

Counting to 10

Count.

0 1 2 ☐ 3 4 5 ☐ 7 ☐ 9 ☐

Matching numbers to objects

Match these numbers by drawing a line.

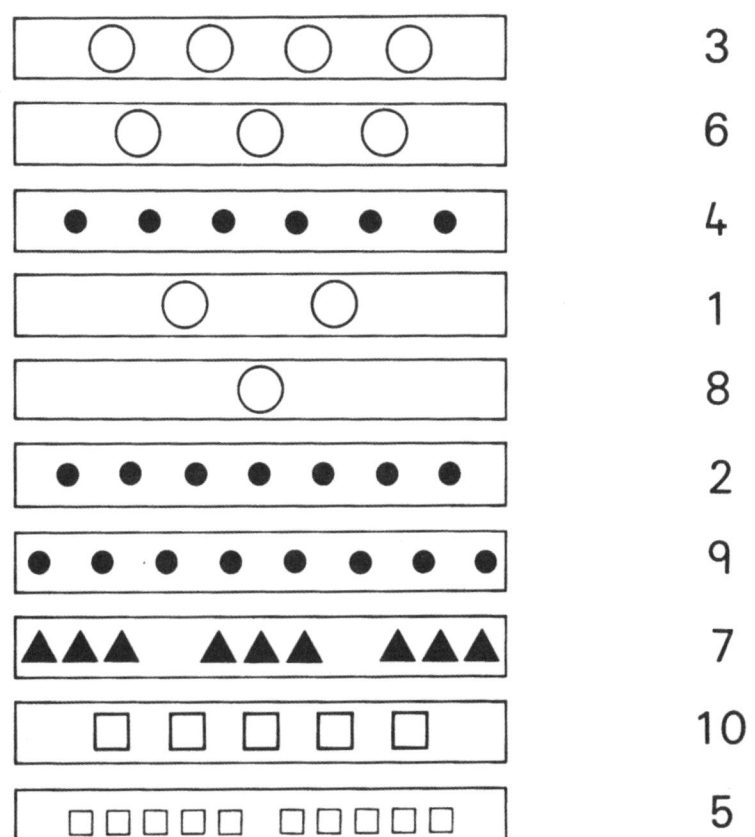

Spelling the number 10

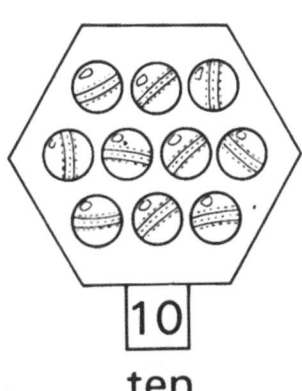

ten

Drawing objects up to 10

Draw the number of objects in each circle.

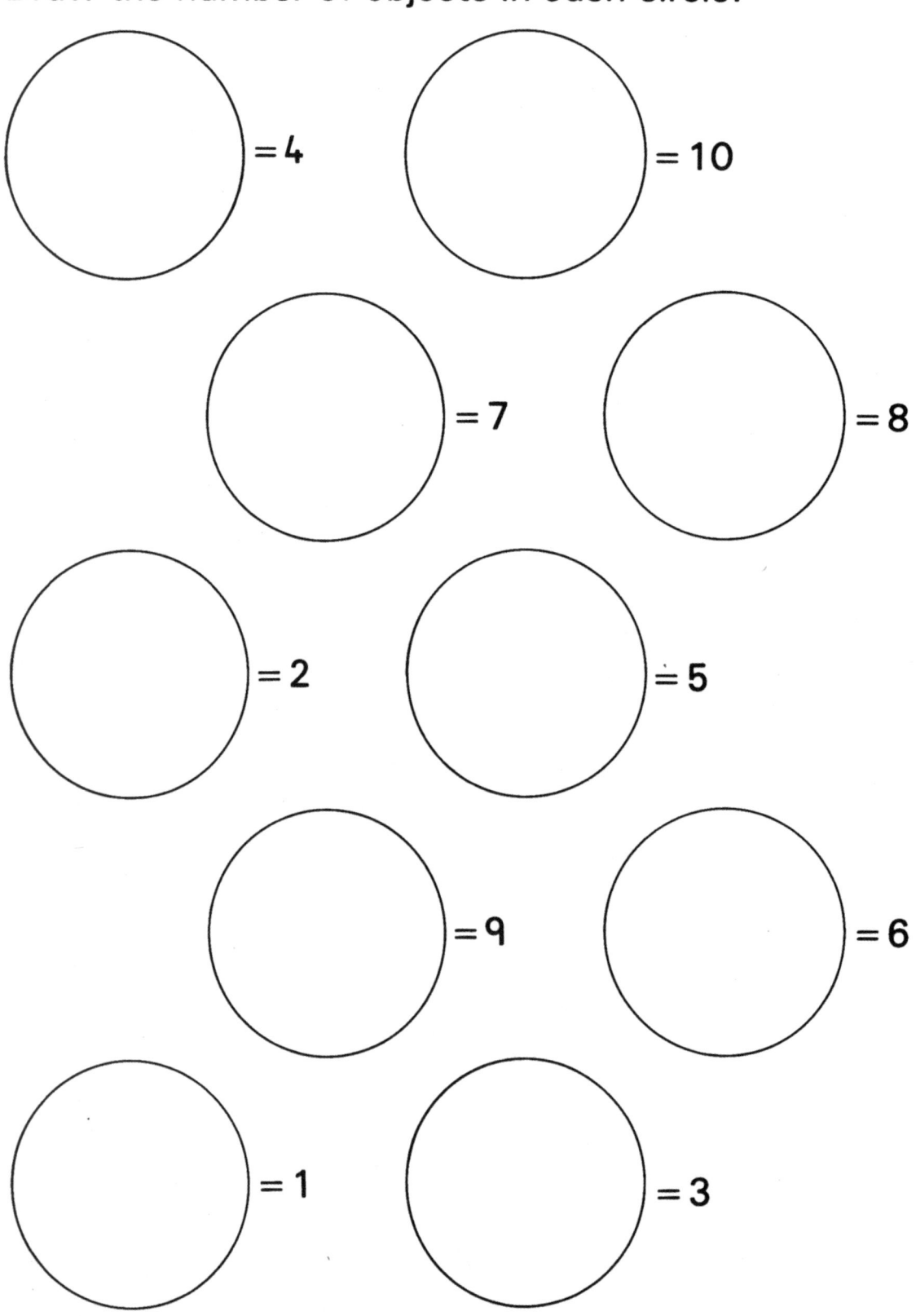

Writing numbers up to 10

Write these numbers.

eight =   two   =

five =   seven =

four =   three =

one   =   zero =

nine =   ten   =

six   =

Counting

	1	2	3	☐	5
	3	4	5	6	☐
	4	☐	6	7	8
	☐	3	4	5	6
	5	☐	7	8	9
	6	7	☐	9	10

Matching

Match one to one.

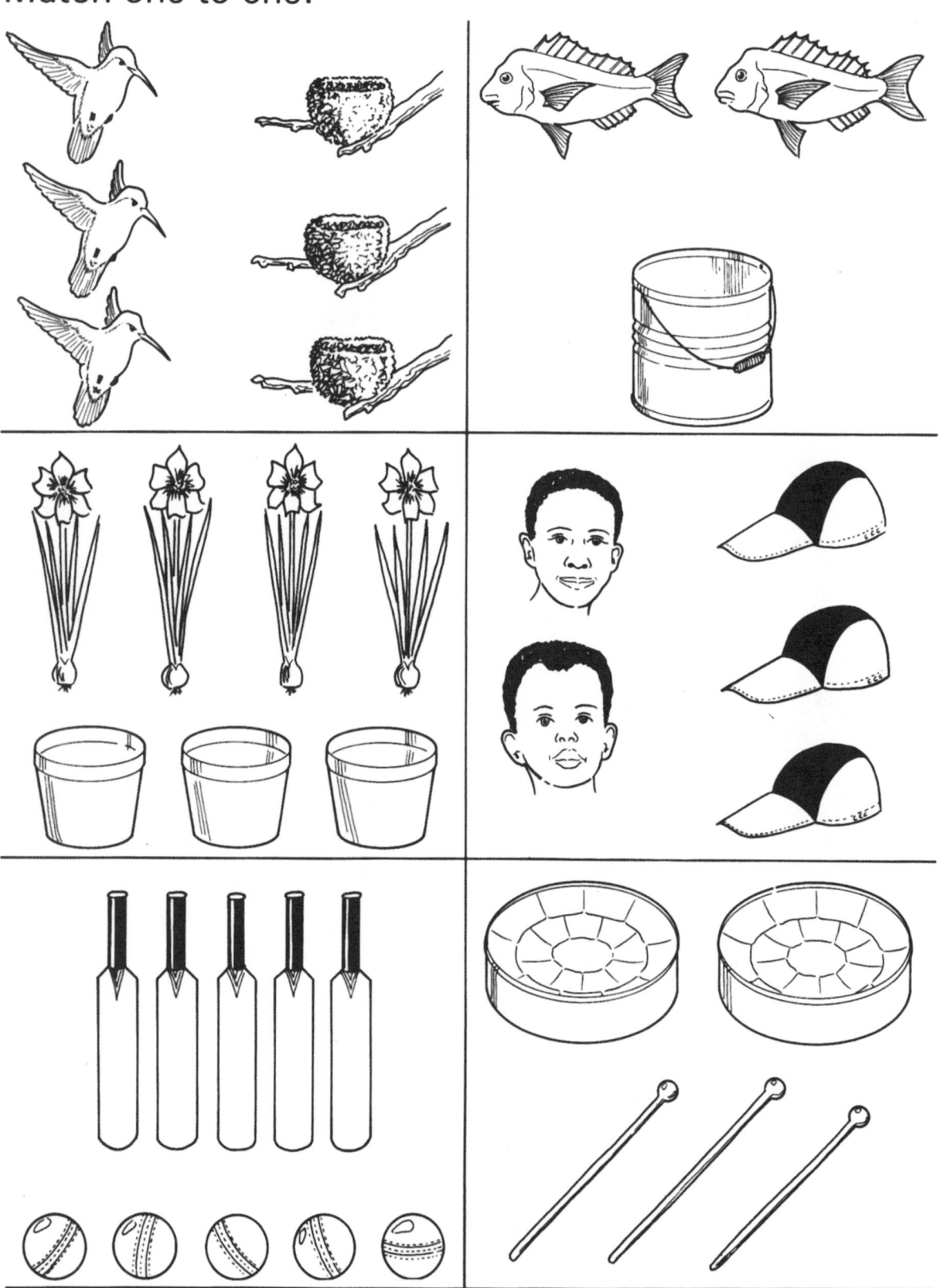

Matching sets

Match sets with the same members.

More

Which is more, A or B? Circle the answer.

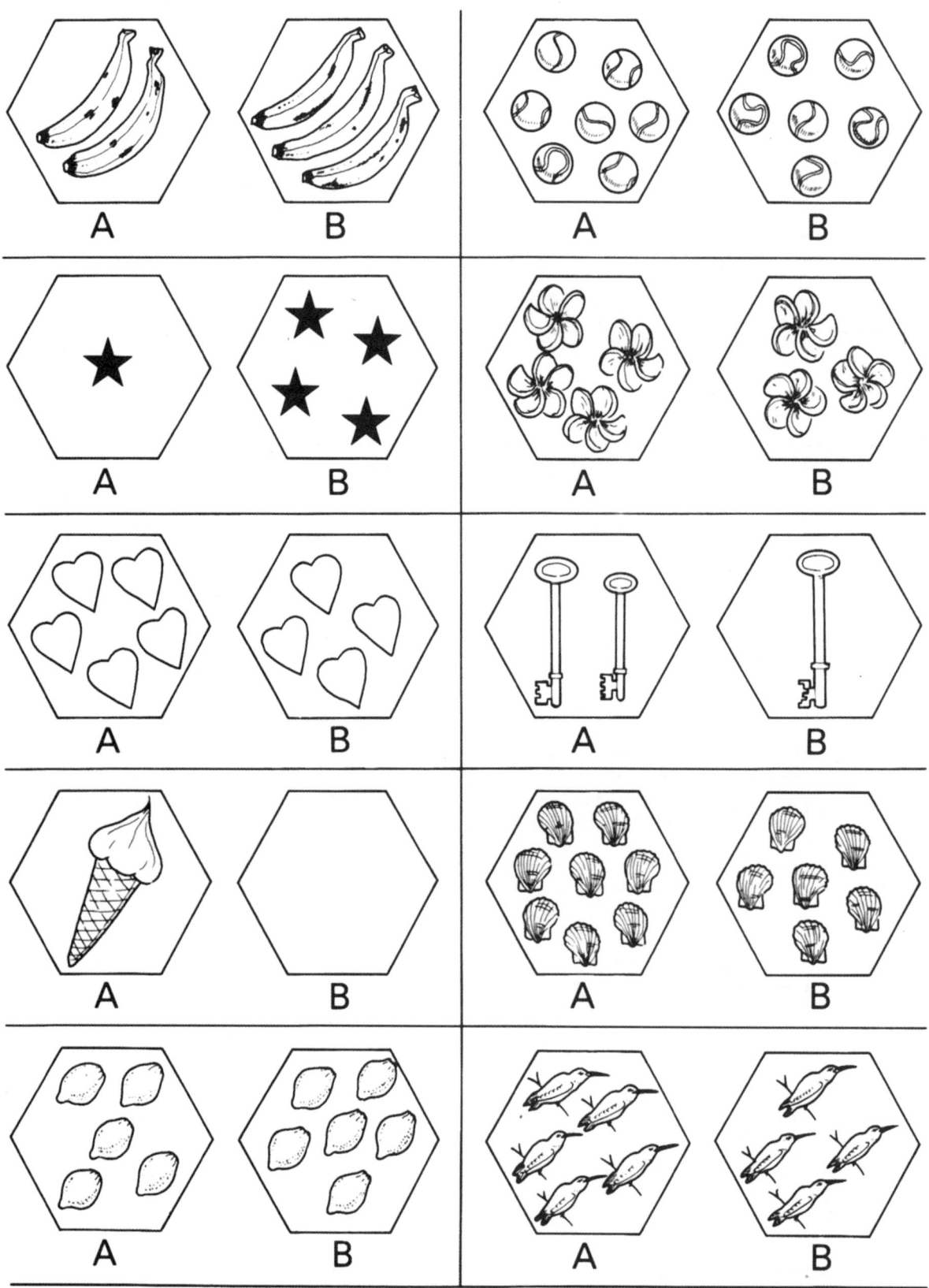

Less

Which is less, A or B? Circle the answer.

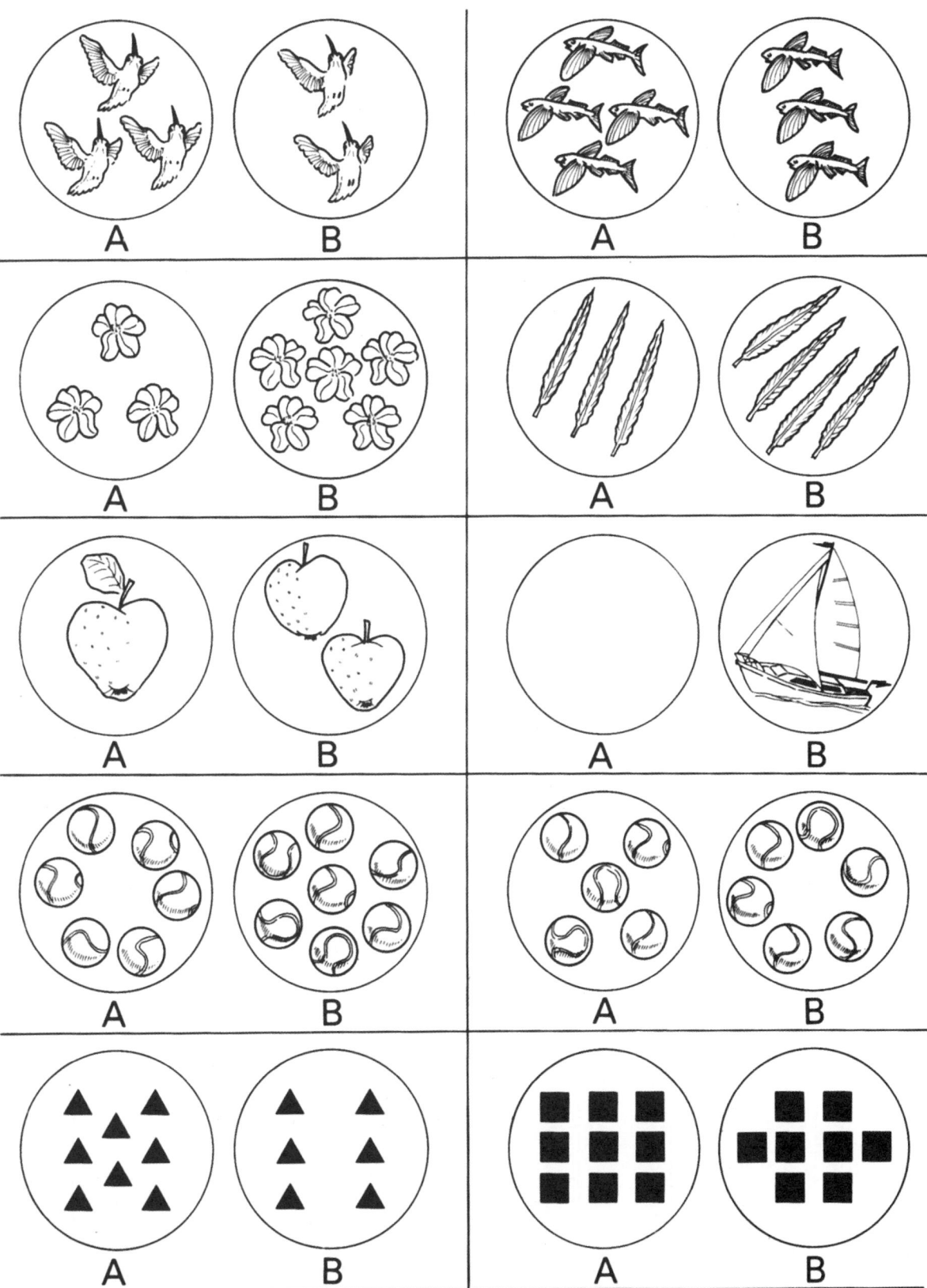

The same as

Which container holds the same as A?

Draw a line to show the same as.

Equal to or the same as

Draw the same number of objects in the circle.

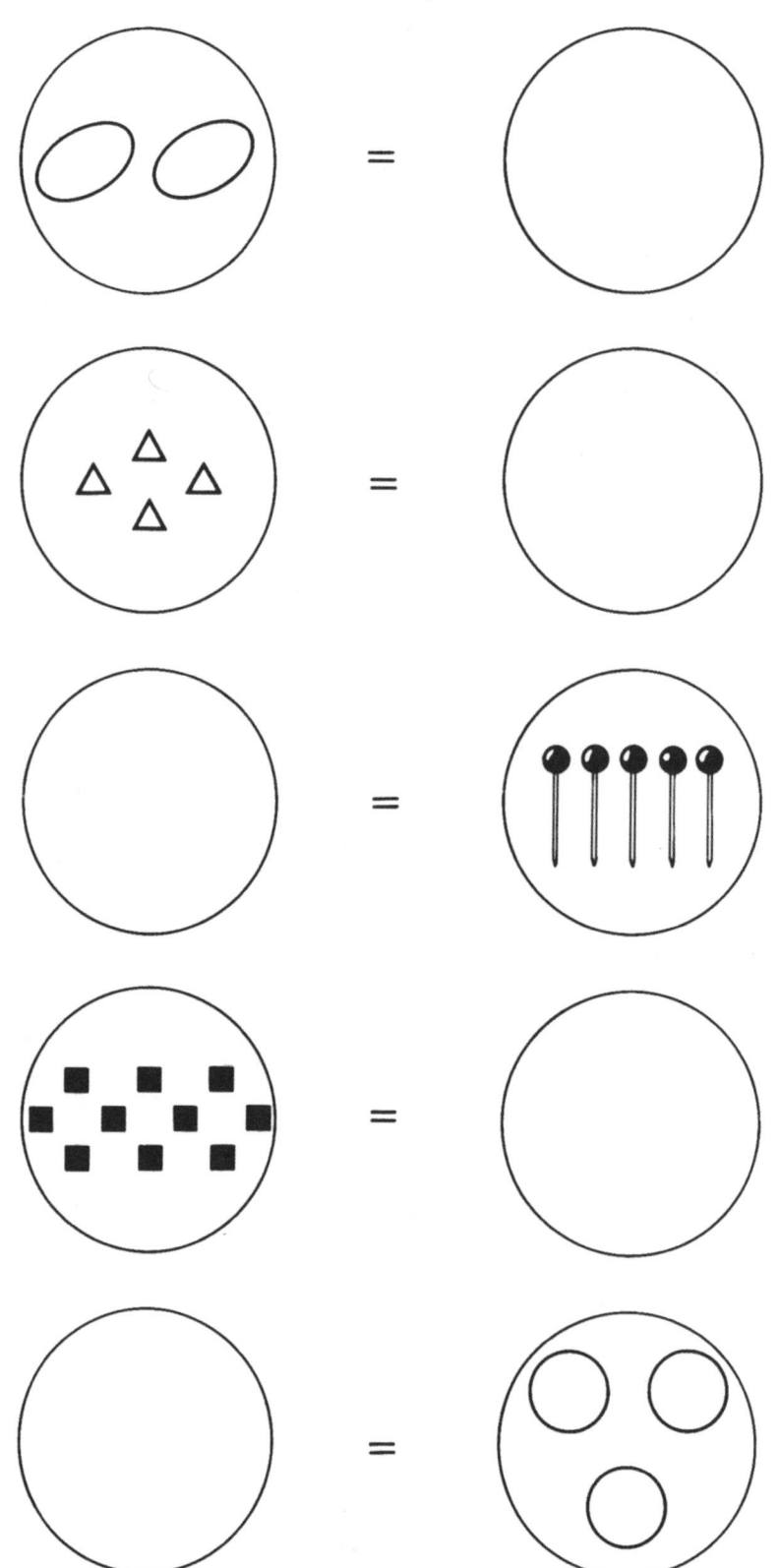